IDEAS BANK
RE
JUDAISM

Elaine McCreery

CONTENTS

Folens Publishers

How to use this book

Ideas Bank books provide ready-to-use, practical, photocopiable activity pages for children, **plus** a wealth of ideas for extension and development.

TEACHER IDEAS PAGE

PHOTOCOPIABLE ACTIVITY PAGE

Clear focus to the activity.

Background information and other help given.

Ways of introducing the subject matter to the children.

Extension activities suggested to take the work one stage further.

Suggestions for developing work on the photocopiable pages.

Independent activities for children to work with.

● Time-saving, relevant and practical, **Ideas Bank** books ensure that you will always have work ready to hand.

Editor: Edward Rippeth
Illustrations: Dandi Palmer

Layout artist: Patricia Hollingsworth
Cover image: Tony Stone Images

Cover design: In Touch Creative Design Ltd

© 1995 Folens Limited, on behalf of the author.

First published 1995 by Folens Limited, Dunstable and Dublin.
Folens Limited, Albert House, Apex Business Centre, Boscombe Road, Dunstable, LU5 4RL, England.

ISBN 1 85276 825-8

Printed in Singapore by Craft Print.

Introduction

This book is designed to help teachers introduce children to the Jewish tradition. On each teacher page there is information about one aspect of Judaism as well as ideas for starting the topic and following it up. The facing page is photocopiable and is intended for the children's use after they have been introduced to the topic.

Current requirements for RE mean that all children are to be introduced to the world's religions. They should develop a knowledge of the main beliefs and traditions, and an ability to reflect on such learning in terms of their own beliefs and experiences. This book aims to bring the two together and so each topic involves the children in some thinking about their own responses to the subjects.

The topics serve as a basic introduction to Judaism upon which further study could be built. They relate closely to the recent model syllabuses produced by SCAA. Each topic involves the teacher in a small amount of preparatory work, and some require the availability of resources, such as a children's Bible.

Teaching about Judaism

Many of the activities in the book draw attention to the fact that for Jewish people, the family and the Torah are important features of their way of life. Teaching about Judaism should reflect this and should strive to present Judaism as a living, modern religion. Teachers should avoid any suggestion that Judaism was somehow replaced by Christianity and should not refer to Judaism in Christian terms. For example, Jews would not refer to their Bible as the 'Old Testament'. Wherever possible, teachers should try to make use of any links they have with Jewish communities to support their teaching. Using visits and visitors will help bring to life the work in the classroom.

Teachers should be aware that many Jews do not refer to the name of God as a mark of respect, and as a result write G-d. Other things to notice are that Hebrew words are used where appropriate – those explained in the glossary are printed in bold. Dating and festivals also reflect the Jewish calendar which is based on a lunar cycle. Jews use this calendar to mark dates of births and deaths.

Jewish Calendar
Tishri (September/October)
Marchevan (October / November)
Kislev (November / December)
Tebet (December / January)
Shebat (January / February)
Adar (February / March)
Nisan (March / April)
Iyyar (April / May)
Sivan (May / June)
Tammuz (June / July)
Ab (July / August)
Ellul (August / September)

Dates of historic events are denoted in this book using CE and BCE (Common Era and Before Common Era), the Common Era beginning with the birth of Jesus.

As with other religions, there are different groups within Judaism and children need to be made aware that there is a variety of observance. The main groups within Judaism are referred to as orthodox and progressive (which includes reform and liberal traditions). Practice and traditions vary between these groups and at appropriate points in the book, the differences are explained.

God – Ideas Page

Aims

- To help children understand the Jewish concept of God as creator of the world.
- To encourage them to reflect on the beauty of the natural world.

How to care for the natural world.

1. Recycle things.

2. Take care of animals and plants.

3. Throw litter into waste bins.

Background

Jewish people believe they have a special relationship with God, dating from the time when Abraham made a covenant (agreement) with Him. From that time onwards, Jews have believed in their special responsibility in the world as God's chosen people. They believe that the world is God's creation and people should obey Him. God cares for everyone and everything, but humans also have a role to care for His world. Jews are taught to respect God's world and wilful destruction of natural resources is prohibited.

God as creator can be seen in the **Tenakh** (the Jewish scriptures), for example in Genesis 1, Psalm 8 and Psalm 148. The festival of **Rosh Hashanah** is a time when Jews remember the creation of the world. The day is referred to as 'the birthday of the world'. During this festival, Jews may eat apples dipped in honey in anticipation of a sweet year ahead.

Starting points

- Show the children pictures of the natural world and talk about what it means to them.
- Ask them what they find beautiful in nature. Discuss places, nearby or abroad, that the children have visited which they think are beautiful.

Activities

- Refer to Genesis 1 in a children's Bible and read or tell it to the children. Ask them to think how they might illustrate this story. Encourage them to consider the words carefully before deciding what to draw.
- Discuss how people, as individuals, can care for each other and the world. This might include disposing of rubbish carefully and not wasting natural resources. Ask them about pollution and conservation. The children could then write or draw their own ideas for a classroom display.

Developments

- Ask the children to paint pictures representing the creation of the world.
- They could collect favourite pictures of the natural world from their own photographs and magazines.
- Ask them to find stories from other traditions which explain the beginning of the world.
- The children could create music to reflect the days of creation.
- Ask them to find out more about the festival of Rosh Hashanah.

Beliefs about God

Jewish people believe God created the world in six days.

● Read the creation stories in Genesis 1 and draw in the four missing days of creation in the circle.

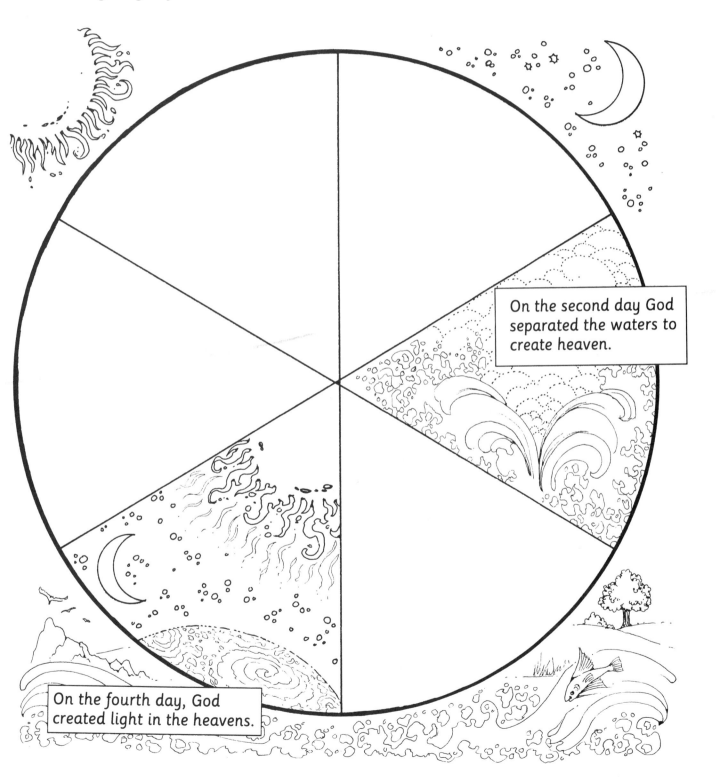

On the second day God separated the waters to create heaven.

On the fourth day, God created light in the heavens.

The Shema – Ideas Page

Aims

- To recognise the importance of the home in Judaism. In this way children will begin to recognise some of the central beliefs of Judaism.
- To appreciate the use of artefacts as reminders of God.

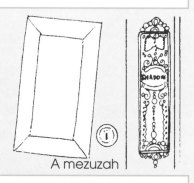

A mezuzah

Starting points

- Discuss objects that are special to the children. Often these things are special because they remind us of somebody.
- If possible, obtain a mezuzah, or a picture of one.

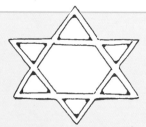

The Star of David

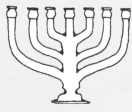

A menorah

Background

Many religions use artefacts or objects which focus their attention on God, as a reminder of His presence, or as a focus for worship. The **Shema** is the central statement of faith for Jews. It identifies Him as the only God, and establishes His relationship with human beings. A copy of the Shema, written on parchment, is kept in a box called a **mezuzah** (meaning 'doorpost'). This is pinned to the door frames in Jewish homes (but not doors into the toilet). It can be made from wood, plastic or metal, and fixing it fulfils the biblical commandment 'You shall write them upon the doorposts of your house and upon thy gates' (Deuteronomy 6:9). Jewish people may touch or kiss the mezuzah on entering the room, as an acknowledgement of God's presence in the home. The front of the mezuzah may be decorated with Jewish symbols and will have the word 'Shaddai' (meaning 'almighty'), or at least the first letter of this word, on the front.

The Shema can also be contained in small black leather boxes called **tefillin** which are tied to the upper arm and forehead for prayer. 'Tie them on your arms and wear them on your foreheads as a reminder' (Deuteronomy 6:8).

> **My special objects**
> 1. The jumper my gran knitted.
> 2. My football boots.

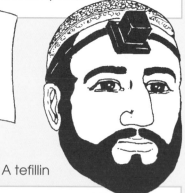

A tefillin

Activities

- Ask the children to read the Shema out loud. It can be found in Deuteronomy 6:4. Talk about what the text means. What is meant by Israel? What does 'The Lord is One' mean?
- Explain to them what a mezuzah is and how it is used.
- Ask the children to think of a suitable design for the front of a mezuzah. Symbols of Judaism such as the Star of David or the **menorah** (a seven-branched candelabra) might be suitable. They will need to put the first letter of Shaddai on the front.

Developments

- Ask the children to make a model of a mezuzah out of clay or card and decorate it.
- They could also research reference books on Judaism to find out about other Jewish reminders of God. These might include the skull-cap or prayer shawl.
- The children might also think about their own home. Do they have any special objects? Why are they special?

The Shema

● This is a shema scroll.

Hear, O Israel,
The Lord our God the Lord is One,
and you shall love the Lord your God
with all your heart and with all
your soul and with all your might.

Deuteronomy 6:4

● Design the front of this mezuzah to keep the Shema in.
  Remember this mezuzah is on its side.

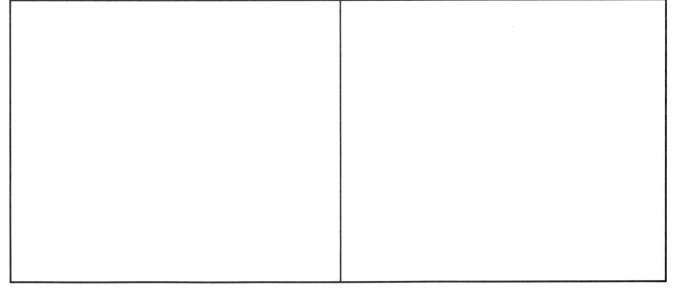

 ● Where do you keep your special things? Draw or
  write about them below.

The Ten Commandments – Ideas Page

Aims

- To consider the idea of having sets of rules to follow.
- To understand that Judaism, like many religions, has a set of rules for its followers. The Ten Commandments form the basis of Jewish law.
- To consider the value of rules to a community.
- To explore the significance of the Ten Commandments for present day living.

Map showing Mt Sinai

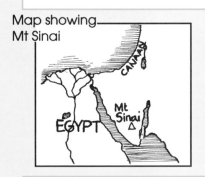

Background

The Ten Commandments lie at the heart of Jewish law. In the Jewish scriptures, the **Torah** gives many rules which apply to all aspects of life. They were compiled to serve the Jewish people during their time of wandering in the desert and are religious in emphasis. The Ten Commandments are believed to have been given to Moses by God, and are of two types – those relating to God and those relating to behaviour.

The scriptures tell of how Moses went up Mount Sinai during the Israelites' time of wandering. No-one else was allowed there while Moses spoke to God. When he came down he brought with him the Ten Commandments. The commandments can be found in Exodus 20.

The Ten Commandments

- You shall have no other gods except me.
- You shall not make graven images.
- You shall not misuse the name of the lord your God.
- Remember the Sabbath day, keeping it holy.
- Honour your father and your mother.
- You shall not murder.
- You shall not commit adultery.
- You shall not steal.
- You shall not give false testimony against your neighbour.
- You shall not covet your neighbour's possessions.

Starting points

- Discuss with the children the rules that they encounter in their own lives, for example, in school, at home and in the wider society. What are the rules? Why are they there? Are some rules different in different places?
- Ask the children why rules are necessary for people to be able to live together. What is the effect on people when rules are broken? Provide a copy of the Ten Commandments for reference, ideally from a children's Bible.

Activities

- Read out each of the commandments and discuss their meaning with the children. Some need to be explained in modern terms for the children to understand them. For example, 'coveting a neighbour's goods' is likely to be very difficult for the children to understand.
- Ask them to study the pictures on the sheet and decide which commandments they refer to.
- Invite the children to make suggestions for pictures for the other commandments.

Developments

- Divide the children into small groups and ask them to make their own sets of commandments. These could be for the class, the school, or even society as a whole. Then compare the sets and choose the best ones for a class list of commandments.
- Look at one particular commandment and ask the children to write about how it could be kept today.

The Ten Commandments

● Which commandments are being kept or broken in the pictures?
● Write your answers in the spaces.

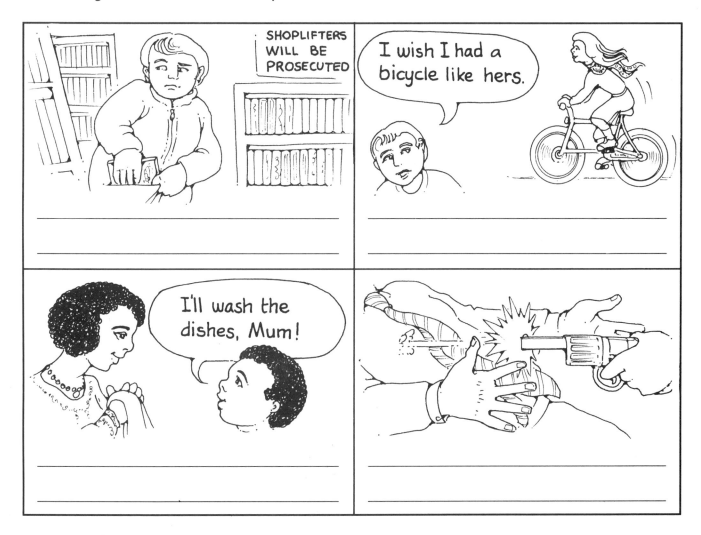

 ● Choose one of the Ten Commandments and draw
a picture showing how people might keep it today.

Commandment _____

Lifestyle – Ideas Page

Aims

- To recognise that a person's lifestyle is influenced by his or her beliefs and commitments.
- To use some of the practices of the Jewish tradition to demonstrate this to the children.
- To show the value of pattern and tradition in a person's life.

Regular events in my life

Lunch	Every day
School	Every day except weekends and holidays
Guides	Once a week
Dentists	Once every six months
Passover	Once a year

Background

The lifestyle of Jewish people is guided by their belief in God and their understanding of the scriptures. There are many patterns within Jewish life which help people to remember their traditions, such as the Sabbath, the festivals and rites of passage. Often, objects are used to help focus attention, particularly in worship. Jewish tradition also includes laws about daily living, including some relating to food.

Common artefacts in Jewish tradition include the following:

- The **kippah** (also known as capel or yamulkah) is a head covering worn during worship. Some followers wear it all the time. It is a sign of respect, recognising the presence of God. In eastern tradition the covering of the head shows respect.
- The **tallit** (or tallith) is a prayer shawl. It is a four-cornered garment with fringes which are knotted to represent the laws of the **Torah**. This originated from Biblical instructions for men to wear fringes on their clothes as reminder of the laws of God.
- **Magen David** (meaning Shield of David) is popularly known as the Star of David. Its origins are not certain, but it is probably the most well-known symbol of Judaism.
- The **menorah** is a seven-branched candelabra which was lit daily in the Temple of ancient Jerusalem. Although Jews use it as a symbol, for example, in pictures and models, it is never lit, as the Temple is no longer there.

Magen David

A menorah

A kippah

A tallit

Starting points

- Ask the children to think about the daily pattern of their life. How do they spend a typical day, week or year? What events happen regularly? A daily event might be school, a weekly event the brownies, an annual event a holiday.
- Ask the children to think of objects they use in their everyday lives, and what they are used for. These might range from simple things like clothes and toys to special things like jewellery and precious belongings.

Activities

- The children could collect pictures of objects used within Jewish tradition and explain what they symbolise.
- Ask the children to make their own design for a kippah. What images could be suitable?
- Discuss with them objects of special significance to different religions. Ask them to write about or draw an object of religious significance to their religion.

Developments

- The children could draw a Jewish man ready for prayer.
- Ask a Jewish person to come into school and explain how the objects help them in their understanding of Judaism.

Remembering God

- Make your own design for this kippah.

- What objects remind you of your god?
- Write about or draw one here.

Abraham – Ideas Page

Aims

- To introduce Abraham as a key figure in the founding of Judaism.
- To recognise his importance in Jewish tradition.
- To locate the geographical origins of Judaism and to consider the implications of commitment to belief.

Reasons for journeying

Refugees	Escaping Prosecution
Hajjis and hajjahs	Pilgrimage

Background

Stories about Abraham can be found in the early books of the Bible and he is recognised as one of the founders of Judaism. Originally named Abram ('exalted father'), he lived in Ur in about 2000BCE (Before Common Era). Ur was a fine city but its people worshipped gods of the sun and moon. Abram's father, Terah, wished to worship in his own way and embarked on a journey with his family to Haran. Abram and some followers came to believe that there was only one true God, and he heard the call of God telling him to leave Haran. He gathered his wife, Sarah, his family, servants, flocks and herds and headed south, without knowing his destination. Abram made a covenant or agreement with God and as a consequence, he changed his name to Abraham ('father of a multitude') and promised that all males would be circumcised. This is the origin of the Jewish claim to the land we know as Israel today.

Starting points

- Discuss the children's experiences of journeys. Where did they go and why did they journey?
- Discuss the fact that people journey for many reasons – sometimes they are forced to, like refugees.
- Introduce the idea that some people journey because of their religious beliefs.
- Encourage the children to reflect on the different feelings associated with journeys for various purposes. A trip to the dentist is probably different from a trip abroad.

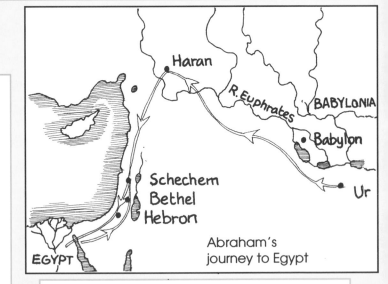

Abraham's journey to Egypt

Developments

- Read other stories about Abraham from the Bible or Jewish reference books.
- Find out about other historical figures who journeyed for religious reasons; for example, Saint Paul in Christian tradition and Muhammad (peace be upon him) in Muslim tradition.
- Make a wall collage showing Abraham's journey and life.

Activities

- Read to or tell the children about Abraham. Suitable stories can be found in Genesis 12 (which describes his journey) and 15–17 (his covenant with God).
- The children will need atlases for the activity. Talk them through the different parts on the map of Israel and surrounding areas. Point out significant features such as rivers or mountains. Some places have changed their names or no longer exist, such as Ur and Canaan.
- They could then complete the map on the activity sheet, using colour to identify land and water.

Abraham's journey

- This is a map of Canaan and Babylon.
- Colour in the land, sea and rivers.
- Use an atlas to put in these missing place names:

  Egypt   River Euphrates

  Red Sea   Dead Sea

  River Tigris   Hebron

- Draw a line on the map to show Abraham's journey (Genesis 12).

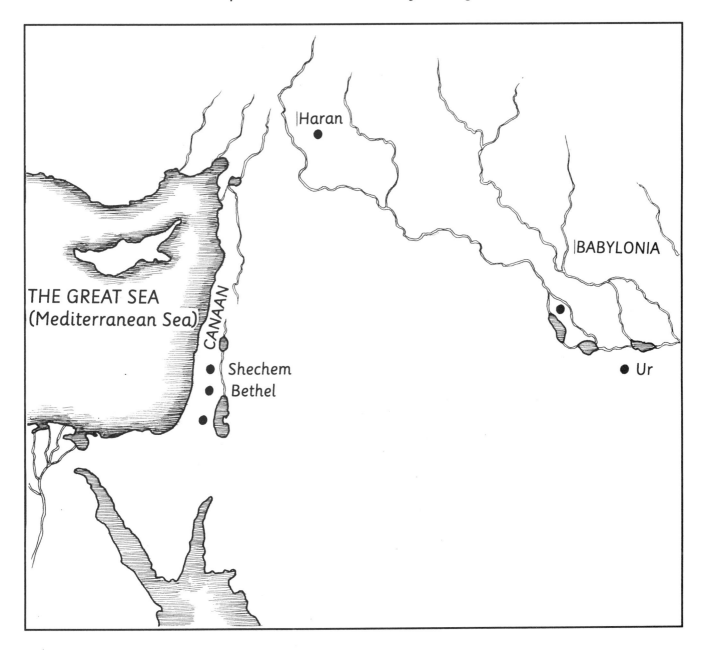

- What are the modern names for these places?

  Canaan   Haran

  Shechem   Bethel

Aims

- To develop the children's knowledge of Moses, one of the key figures in Judaism.
- To appreciate that Jewish people trace their history through the stories in the **Tenakh**. The concept of God working to defeat evil is also established.

My baby stories

1. I was the loudest baby in the ward.

2. I was born ten minutes after my twin.

Starting points

- Ask the children what they know about their own early life. When and where were they born? What details do they know about where they lived? What were they like as babies? Perhaps they have been told some interesting stories about their life as a baby, by their parents and relatives.
- Ask them what they know about Moses. They may be aware of the stories of his early life and the escape from Egypt. How did they know about these stories? Were they told them, did they see them on television, or did they read about them?
- Read or tell them the story of Moses' early years in Exodus 1–2.

Background

Stories about the early life of key religious figures are common to many traditions, such as Jesus and Buddha. Moses was linked by birth to the earlier founders of Judaism, but was brought up by Egyptians – the oppressors of the Hebrews. The Hebrews had moved to Egypt during a time of famine and had settled there. However, they were enslaved by the Egyptians and forced to build their cities.

At the time of Moses' birth, the Egyptian Pharaoh had ordered the death of all male babies to control the growing number of Hebrews. Moses was saved by being placed in a basket and put on the river Nile. He was found and adopted by the Pharaoh's daughter, and was brought up as an Egyptian. Although brought up in luxury, Moses never forgot that he was a Hebrew. As an adult, he killed an Egyptian who was mistreating a Hebrew slave. He fled from Egypt, but while in hiding, he heard the voice of God telling him to return to free the Hebrews.

Exodus, Leviticus, Numbers and Deuteronomy describe how Moses helped to free the Hebrews, gave them laws to live by and eventually led them to the Promised Land.

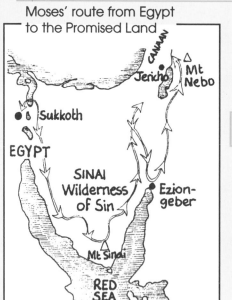

Moses' route from Egypt to the Promised Land

Enslavement in Egypt

Activities

- Discuss with the children the roles of different people in the story. Encourage the children to think about their motives.
- The children could write about each person in their own words.

Developments

- Read further stories about the life of Moses. For example, God's call to Moses (Exodus 2–3); the deliverance from Egypt (Exodus 5–12); the Ten Commandments (Exodus 19–20); the death of Moses (Deuteronomy 34).
- Discuss slavery – are there still people today who might be thought of as 'slaves'?
- Talk about the story of Moses' birth. Why was it considered important?

The story of Moses

- Who are these people and what did they do in the story?
  Why did they do these things?

- Write your answers in the spaces under the drawings.

Pharaoh

Pharaoh's daughter

Moses' mother

Moses' sister

Moses

Aims

- To introduce the children to the roles and work of the rabbi within the Jewish community.
- To consider where and how people learn about different aspects of life.
- To consider authority – who people trust to tell the truth.

A rabbi with Torah scrolls

Background

Rabbi comes from a Hebrew word meaning '**teacher**'. An important part of a rabbi's work is teaching people about the Jewish way of life. In progessive Jewish tradition, there are an increasing number of female rabbis. The rabbi should have an understanding of the scriptures and other Jewish writings and should know the details of Jewish observance in order to advise the community. Rabbis are also concerned with their congregation's welfare and often visit hospitals to comfort the sick. They lead the synagogue worship and special ceremonies like Bar Mitzvahs, weddings and funerals.

There is much academic training in preparation for the job, but experience of life is also vital. Rabbis are expected to set an example by their behaviour, and to marry and have children. Rabbis are not required to wear special clothes for services but are likely to wear the prayer shawl and capel. A group of rabbis can form a Beth Din (house of law) to decide matters of Jewish law, such as the licensing of **kosher** butchers, conversions to Judaism and divorce.

Activities

- Discuss with the children how a rabbi might help all members of his or her community, such as children, old or sick people and people who wish to learn more about their faith. In Judaism, as in other faiths, the link between a person's physical welfare and spiritual welfare is important.
- Ask the children to suggest answers for the pictures on the sheet. What could the rabbi be teaching, and what kind of comfort could he provide?
- Ask them to complete the final list themselves and then compare answers with each other.

Starting points

- Discuss with the children the people who teach us. What do we learn from different people? What do we learn from our parents, family, friends, teachers, books and television?
- Talk about where religious people find out about their faith, for example home, place of worship, scriptures, other people.

RABBI WANTED

We are looking for:

- *An enthusiastic member of the Jewish faith.*
- *Somebody familiar with Jewish law and tradition.*
- *A caring and kind person.*
- *A good teacher.*
- *Married candidates are preferred.*

Developments

- Invite a rabbi into school to talk about his or her work.
- Write a job advert for a rabbi describing the skills and qualities which would make a person suitable for the role.
- Encourage the children to think of why a person might wish to become a rabbi.
- Find out about rabbis who are well-known today, such as Rabbi Lionel Blue and Rabbi Julia Neuberger.

The work of a rabbi

● How might a rabbi help these people? Write your answers in the spaces next to the pictures.

Visiting someone in hospital

_____

_____

_____

_____

_____

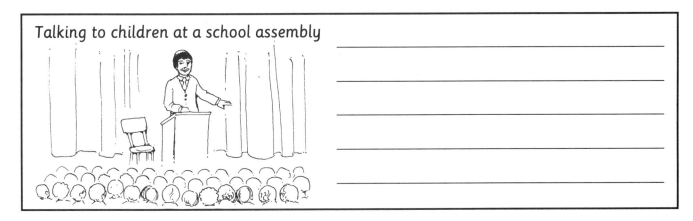

Talking to children at a school assembly

_____

_____

_____

_____

_____

Teaching adults at the synagogue

_____

_____

_____

_____

_____

NOW ● What kind of person should a rabbi be?
Think of some words to add to this list.

helpful _____ _____

friendly _____ _____

Home and Shabbat – Ideas Page

Aims

- To appreciate the importance of the Sabbath in a Jewish home.
- To consider the importance of having time for reflection.

Background

Jews believe that God created the world in six days and rested on the seventh. The fourth commandment says, 'Remember the Sabbath (or **Shabbat** in Hebrew) to keep it holy. In it thou shalt not do any work'. The Sabbath begins at Friday sunset and ends Saturday sunset. Before it begins, the home is cleaned and food is prepared. No work is done on the Sabbath. Some orthodox Jews refuse to do simple tasks that progressive Jews would do, for example switching lights on. The Sabbath is used as a time to spend with the family, to think of God and to make a special day different from the usual working day.

Lit candles welcome the Sabbath

Challah (plaited loaf) is eaten

A cup of wine is drunk

Starting points

- Ask the children how they spend the weekend. Do they play, go shopping or go to a place of worship? Is it a relaxing time? What things do they do with their family? Are there times when the whole family get together?
- Discuss the children's favourite times at home. It could be watching television, being alone in their room, or perhaps playing with brothers and sisters.

My favourite time is with my friends playing computer games.

My favourite time is lying in on Saturday mornings.

Activities

- Tell the children about the Jewish Sabbath, its importance to Jews and how they spend it. Emphasise the importance of the family spending time together and setting a day aside to think of God. Discuss the work that needs to be done in a home before the Sabbath begins. Cooking, cleaning and washing-up have to be done, so that nothing needs to be done on the Sabbath.
- Ask the children which activities can be done on the Sabbath and which can not. What constitutes work in the children's eyes? The children could complete the sheet with their own suggestions. When they have finished, they could compare their answers. Discuss any disagreements.

Developments

- Ask the children how they would spend their perfect day. Where would they go? What would they do?
- Ask them to compare a Jewish child's Sabbath with how others spend the weekend.
- Read the creation story, in which God creates the world and then rests on the seventh day (Genesis 1 and 2).
- Talk about the value of a family getting together regularly.

My perfect day
1. Play netball.
2. Watch my favourite programme on T.V.
3. Go to a burger bar for dinner.

Shabbat – the Sabbath

● What jobs need to be done before the Sabbath begins?
  Fill in the list below.

Jobs to do:

_____   _____

_____   _____

_____   _____

_____   _____

_____   _____

● Which of these activities are good ways to spend the Sabbath?
  Which should not be done? For each activity put a tick or a
  cross in the box and explain why over the page.

● In the last empty box, draw an activity that can be done on
  the Sabbath.

1. Shopping

2. Homework

3. Being with the family

4. Eating

5. Going to the synagogue

6. _____

Home and food – Ideas Page

Aims

- To recognise the importance of the home in Jewish tradition.
- To consider what is special about the place people call 'home'.
- To understand the importance of the food laws to Jews and the implications of these in the home.

What I learn at home
1. Good manners.
2. How to do chores, like washing up.

Starting points

- Discuss with the children what a home is. Home can mean different things to different people. What is the difference between talking about 'my house' and 'my home'?
- Ask the children to think about what they learn at home. This might include references to behaviour, belief, manners, how to look after a home, living with people.
- Discuss the traditions people have in their home, such as families gathering for regular events like meals.

Our family has a roast every Sunday

Our family visits our aunt in Scotland every summer

Background

The Jewish home is a very special place and more than a place to live. It is central to keeping traditions alive and protecting the community for the future. Many of the important festivals are celebrated in the home. This reflects the turbulent history of the Jewish people, who, when living in sometimes hostile countries, needed the home as a secure place in which to practise their faith. One of the most significant features of the Jewish home is the treatment of food. Jews should eat only **kosher** or 'fit' food. The rules governing eating are to be found in the Bible (Leviticus 11:1–23).

- Meat – only animals that chew the cud and have cloven hoofs may be eaten.
- Sea creatures – only those with fins and scales may be eaten.
- Birds – no birds of prey may be eaten.
- Meat and milk – should not be eaten at the same time. This means that meat and milk produce will be kept separately and wherever possible separate pots and utensils will be used for each. Wealthy, orthodox Jews might even have separate kitchens for milk and meat.

Activities

- Talk the children through the rules regarding food, using reference to Leviticus 11:1–23 where necessary. Discuss why certain foods might be considered unfit to eat. The animals that can be eaten are herbivores. Mixing meat and milk is prohibited (tradition forbids cooking a kid in its own mother's milk).
- Talk through the foods on the sheet and ask the children why each may or may not be eaten.
- Ask them to devise a suitable menu for a Jewish family based on what they know about the rules. They could compare their menus afterwards. Which looks the most appetising?

Animals for kosher food

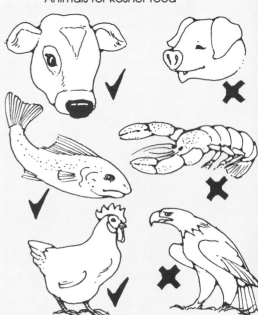

Developments

- Discuss which animals are not considered as food in this country, for example dogs and horses, and why this may be so.

Kosher food

● Which of these foods are Jewish people allowed to eat?
  In the spaces explain why.

Lamb chops

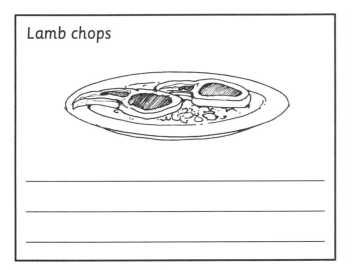

_____

_____

_____

Chicken curry and rice

_____

_____

_____

Ham and mushroom pizza

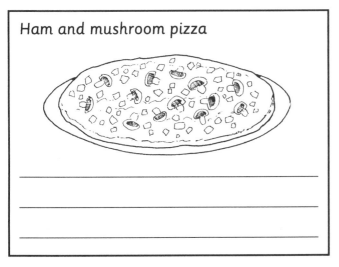

_____

_____

_____

Oysters

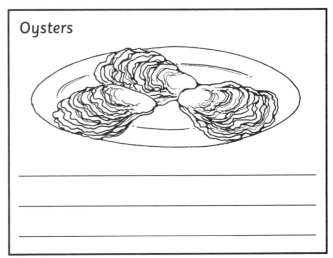

_____

_____

_____

 ● Plan a meal for a Jewish family.
● Write your menu in the spaces below.

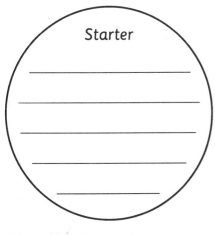

Starter

_____

_____

_____

_____

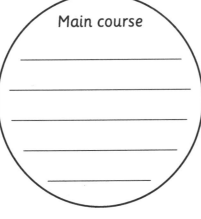

Main course

_____

_____

_____

_____

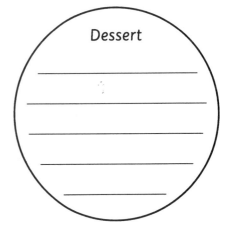

Dessert

_____

_____

_____

_____

Synagogue – Ideas Page

Aims

- To introduce children to the significant features of a synagogue.
- To appreciate the significance of the synagogue for the Jewish community.
- To reflect on significant places in the children's own lives.

Special Places
1. My bedroom
2 Wembley stadium
3. My local synagogue

Starting points

- Talk about the places that are important in the children's lives, such as their home or places they visit. Ask them why it is special, what they do there and how they feel to be there.
- Ask them what they know about places of worship and how they are used.
- Show them a picture of a synagogue and ask why it is special to Jewish people.

Background

Synagogue is a Greek word meaning 'meeting place'. Synagogues became meeting places for Jews after the destruction of the Temple of Jerusalem in 70CE when the Jews were dispersed around the world.

A synagogue is a place of worship which has a number of other purposes for the community. It is used for prayer, for reading and teaching about the law, and for special occasions such as weddings. Social groups often meet there, such as youth clubs. The most important feature of the synagogue is the **Ark** where the **Torah** scrolls are kept. This is a cupboard, usually enclosed by a curtain and doors. It is kept closed and is only opened to take out the Torah scrolls. The Torah scrolls are believed to contain the word of God; Torah means 'law' or 'teaching'.

The building is usually rectangular and seating is on three sides facing the reading stand or **bimah**. There may be separate seating for women in orthodox synagogues. Decorations are generally abstract, as any attempt to represent figures would break the second commandment about graven images.

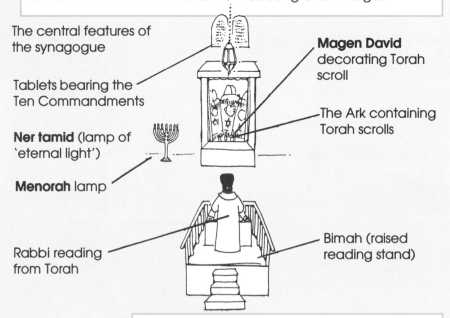

The central features of the synagogue

Tablets bearing the Ten Commandments

Ner tamid (lamp of 'eternal light')

Menorah lamp

Rabbi reading from Torah

Magen David decorating Torah scroll

The Ark containing Torah scrolls

Bimah (raised reading stand)

Activities

- Ask the children how much they know about the various parts of the synagogue, such as the bimah, ark, seating and ner tamid (eternal light), which is a symbol of the presence of God and is kept burning constantly.
- Ask them to research the objects on the sheet and write about them.

Developments

- Ask the children to compare the synagogue with a building used in another religion. What objects could be found there?
- Plan a visit to a synagogue so that the children can see at first-hand the objects they have learned about.
- Invite a Jewish visitor to talk to the children about the role of the synagogue in their community.

Inside a synagogue

● Match the pictures to the labels. Find out what they are used
for and write about them below the pictures.

Ner Tamid (eternal light)	Torah scrolls	Menorah lamp

Magen David	Bimah reading stand	The Ark

Israel – Ideas Page

Aims

- To recognise and appreciate the significance of Israel within Judaism.
- To consider why places are special to different people. From their own experiences the children may be able to identify places which are important to them.

How Israel is different

It is hotter and drier.

The landscape is less green.

It is a 'new' country.

Background

Israel literally means 'one who struggles with God' and can refer to the worldwide Jewish community, the land of Israel or the modern state of Israel. Israel is a special place for all Jews and many visit or go to live there. Many Jews choose to be buried in Israel when they die. The most sacred place for Jews within Israel is Jerusalem, where the ancient Temple stood.

Much of Jewish history, as recorded in the Bible, centres on Israel, and many important events took place in its towns and cities. In modern times, the area has been a place of conflict since it was named the state of Israel in 1948. The Palestinians remain angry that Israel was given back to the Jews (who had dispersed to places all over the world) when they had lived there for generations. The struggle to find a peaceful solution continues today.

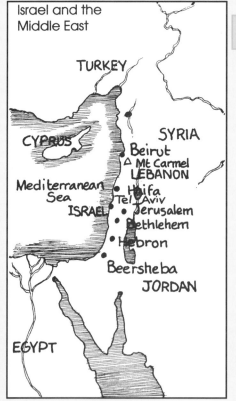

Israel and the Middle East

Activities

- Ask the children to find Israel on a globe or map. They could discuss its location in relation to the Middle East, Europe and the rest of the world.
- Ask them how Israel is likely to be different from their own country, for example, the weather, landscape and food.
- They could then complete the map and discuss why Israel is special to Jewish families. Encourage them to think of the history of Judaism, especially stories relating to Abraham and Moses found in Genesis and Exodus.

Starting points

- Ask the children if there are any places which are special to them. Start the conversation by giving them an example.
- The children's parents or grandparents may originate from other towns, countries or continents. Do they know where these places are? What have they been told about them? Do their parents ever go back there or have they been themselves?
- Collect pictures of modern Israel from magazines and holiday brochures.

Developments

- Collect food labels from produce originating in Israel, such as fruit.
- Invite a Jewish person who has been to Israel to talk to the children about his or her visit.
- Ask the children to write about the place where their families originate.
- They could write about places that are special to them.

Israel

- This map shows Israel.
- Using an atlas, find these places and write them on your map.

  Dead Sea   Hebron   Nazareth   Haifa
  Tel Aviv   River Jordan   Mount Carmel   Jerusalem
  Gaza   Beer Sheba   Bethlehem

- Colour in the land, sea and rivers.

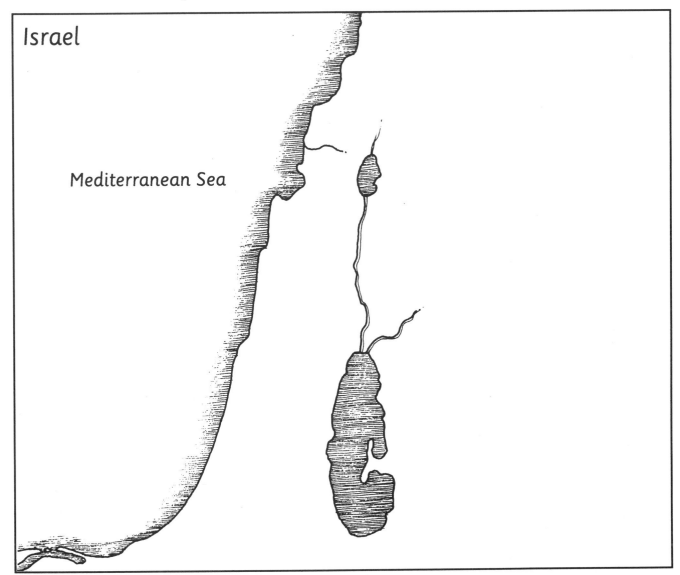

Israel

Mediterranean Sea

- Imagine you had to leave your own country.
  What things would you miss about it?

_____

_____

_____

The Torah – Ideas Page

Aims

- To appreciate the significance of the Torah for Jewish people.
- To consider how a person's beliefs can inform the way they live.

Who I am nice to.
1. My friends.
2. My family.
3. Teachers.
4. Older people.

Starting point

- Ask the children why they know how to behave, in particular how they treat other people. Who are they nice to? This might include family and friends, but what about other people? Who do they help – anyone who needs it? Explain that beliefs inform behaviour.

Background

The term **Torah** means 'law' or 'teaching', and refers to the Five Books of Moses (the first five books of the Bible). It can also mean the **Tenakh** (the Jewish Bible) or the whole of Jewish law.

The laws are believed to have been received by Moses on Mount Sinai. Orthodox Jews consider the Torah to be the living word of God, which is not open to change or interpretation. Progressive Jews are more likely to interpret the Torah, where necessary, for modern living. They believe that it was compiled many years ago for a different time and place. In the **synagogue**, the **Sefer Torah** is the scroll on which the Five Books of Moses are written.

Genesis tells of the creation of the world and the early history of humankind including the figures of Abraham, Jacob and Isaac. Exodus records the delivery of the Israelites and the journey to the Promised Land. Leviticus contains laws about sacrifice in the sanctuary and Numbers follows the wandering of the Jews for 40 years. There are 613 laws and commandments in the Torah, which address many aspects of life. One of the key teachings is 'You shall love your neighbour as yourself' (Leviticus 19:18) which means 'love your fellow humans'.

The Torah is read in the synagogue at each **Shabbat** so that the whole thing is read in the course of a year .

Loving your neighbour as yourself...

Activities

- Using copies of the Bible, locate and name the first five books.
- Find Leviticus 19:18 and discuss what it might mean to love your neighbour as yourself. Ask the children how they can love other people as much as they love themselves? What kinds of things might this involve?
- Ask them to consider who their neighbours are. The people next door or in the same street, people they like or all people?
- They could draw pictures to show how they could put this into practice and then label the books.

Developments

- Organise a fund-raising activity for a charity of the children's choice. A sponsored event or jumble sale might be appropriate.
- Examine other sections of the Torah, such as Deuteronomy, to find other instructions for living.
- Organise a role-play in which the children demonstrate loving your neighbour.

The Torah

Leviticus 19:18 says:
'You shall love your neighbour as yourself.'

● Draw pictures to show how you might love your neighbour.

 ● Use the Bible to find its first five books, and write their names on the books below.

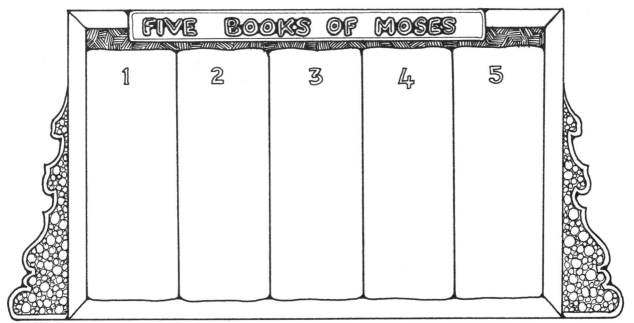

FIVE BOOKS OF MOSES

1 2 3 4 5

Hebrew – Ideas Page

Aims

- To introduce the children to Hebrew, the special language of Judaism.
- To appreciate that Jewish children need to learn the language in order to read the scriptures.

Background

Hebrew is the language of the Jewish scriptures and is one of the world's oldest languages. It is used in **synagogue** services, and the **Torah** is always read in Hebrew. Hebrew is considered to be a vital link with the past, and a way of unifying contemporary Judaism. It is written from right to left in a unique alphabet with no vowel representation. Jewish children learn Hebrew from a young age so that they can begin to read the scriptures. By the time children come of age and become **Bar** or **Bat Mitzvah** (son or daughter of the law) they should be fluent enough to read the scriptures aloud in the synagogue.

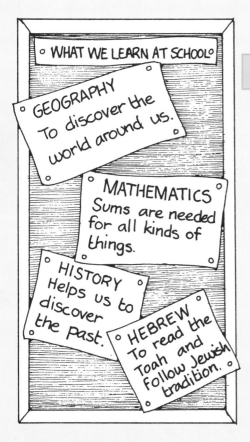

Starting points

- Talk about the different subjects the children learn about in school. What subjects do they study and why are they necessary?
- Ask them about the things they learn outside school. Discuss the groups they attend outside school, such as brownies, cubs or sports clubs, where they learn very specific skills. Let them discuss each others' skills and achievements.
- Ask them if they know a language other than English. Where did they learn this? They may have learned other languages from their parents. Point out that many people never achieve bilingualism.

I am a Cub, and I can put up a tent.

I am a Brownie, and I can ride a pony.

Activities

- Collect some examples of written Hebrew to show the children and ask them what they notice. How is it different from their own alphabet? They will notice that Hebrew books appear 'back to front' because the text is read from right to left.
- Talk about why Jews think Hebrew is so valuable to their traditions (the ancient scriptures were written in Hebrew).
- Talk through the alphabet, noting differences with English. Which letters sound similar, which are different?
- The children could use the alphabet to write their names and those of friends.

Developments

- Discuss other religions that use special languages, such as Islam (Arabic) and Hinduism (Sanskrit).
- Find out what children from other religious backgrounds need to learn about their own traditions.

RELIGIOUS LANGUAGES

Arabic — Islam
Sanskrit — Hinduism
Punjabi — Sikhism
Latin — Catholicism

Hebrew

This is the Hebrew alphabet.

Hebrew	Sound	Hebrew	Sound	Hebrew	Sound
אבגדהוזח	– B G D H V Z Ch	טיכלמנס	T Y K L M N S	פצקרשת	– P/F Tz K R S T

This is the beginning of the Shema which is found inside a mezuzah.

שמע ישראל ה' אלקינו ה' אחד

It means:　　　　Hear O Israel, The Lord our God
　　　　　　　　The Lord is One.

● Copy it on to this scroll. Remember that Hebrew
　is written right to left!

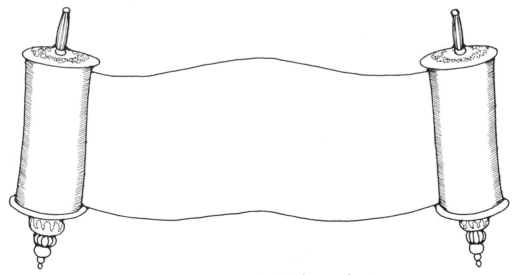

● Write your own name in Hebrew letters.
　Remember there are no vowel letters!

Aims

- To help children recognise the Ark as the central feature of the synagogue.
- To make them aware that symbolism is an important aspect of religion.
- To appreciate that some objects are considered holy and need to be treated with respect.

Starting points

- Ask the children what things are precious to them, and why.
- Collect pictures of the Ark in a synagogue.
- Discuss how people find out about God, and the role of the scriptures and teachers in doing this.
- Ask them about the symbols they see in their daily lives – such as road signs or company logos.

Activities

- Read or tell the children about the Temple priest's special clothing in Exodus 39:1–21.
- Ask the children to match the items from the priest's clothes to the scroll.

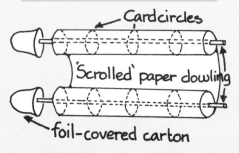

Cardcircles

'Scrolled' paper dowling

foil-covered carton

Background

The **Ark** in a **synagogue** is named after the Ark of the Covenant which held the Ten Commandments in Moses' time. The Ark contains one or more **Sefer Torah** on which are written the Five Books of Moses; Genesis, Exodus, Leviticus, Numbers and Deuteronomy. The Sefer Torah are handwritten on parchment in Hebrew. The scrolls are 'dressed' in symbolic objects and the text is too sacred to be touched by hand. The 'dress' of the scrolls recalls the robes of the Temple priests in ancient times.

A breast-plate is hung over the scroll, usually made from silver. It contains the date to show where the reading is up to.

Features of the Ark

A yad is a hand-held pointer which marks the place in the Sefer Torah's text, to avoid touching it by hand. It is made from wood, silver or any material not used in weapons.

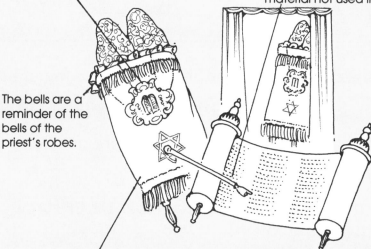

The bells are a reminder of the bells of the priest's robes.

The mantle is reminiscent of the priest's robes and is often made from rich material like velvet to suggest kingship. It helps protect the delicate parchment.

A typical Ark curtain is decorated with Jewish symbols and Hebrew writing. Above it, there is usually a statement written in Hebrew, for example, 'Know before whom you are standing'.

Developments

- Arrange a visit to a synagogue to look specifically at the Ark and the Sefer Torah.
- Ask the children to make models of the scrolls using paper, foil, yoghurt cartons, a pencil, wooden dowelling and some cloth. Roll the paper into a scroll, and insert the dowelling at each end. Place circles of card over the dowelling to keep the shape of the scroll. Cover the yogurt cartons with foil to make 'bells' and attach these to the ends of the dowelling . Make an embroidered cover from cloth with appropriate symbols. Complete the scroll with a breast-plate (foil-covered card) and a yad (a foil-covered pencil).

Inside the Ark

● Match the labels to the correct part of the Sefer Torah.

Yad   Breast-plate   Mantle   Bells

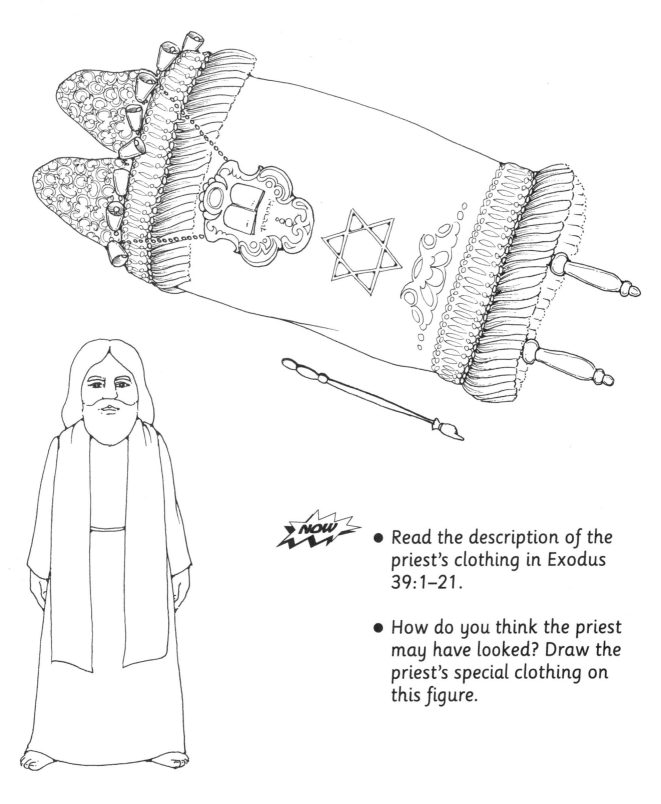

● Read the description of the priest's clothing in Exodus 39:1–21.

● How do you think the priest may have looked? Draw the priest's special clothing on this figure.

The scribe – Ideas Page

Aims

- To understand the role of the scribe in Jewish tradition.
- To consider people who have a special job to do, reflecting on the dedication and hard work that goes into doing a good job.

Starting points

- Show the children some pictures of a Sefer Torah (Torah scroll) and ask them how it could be made. Is it made by a machine or by hand? What materials are used? How is it different from the reading materials we use? Encourage the children to give reasons for their answers.
- Select a passage from the first five books of the Bible, such as Genesis 1 and 2 (the Creation), Genesis 6–9 (Noah), Genesis 37–49 (Joseph), Exodus (Moses) or Deuteronomy 5 (the Ten Commandments) for them to write out.

Background

The scribe (**sofer**) is a significant person in Jewish tradition, as he is trained over several years to write the **Sefer Torah**. It can take five years to write one Torah scroll. The scroll is very long and is made from parchment (animal skin), in sections which are sown together. The text is written in columns and reads from right to left. No base metals can be used – weapons are made from these. The scribe's quill is made from a turkey feather. The ink is specially prepared and dries slowly and smudges easily. The name of God, being so holy, is written throughout the scroll at a separate time from the rest.

Other tools used by the scribe include a **sargel** made from a thorn, used to scratch lines on the parchment; a glass tool to scrape off mistakes, and a silver needle and thimble for sewing. Sinew is used as thread. The scribe also repairs damaged scrolls, writes sections of the Torah on parchment for tefillins and mezuzahs, and makes the black leather boxes of the tefillin.

The scribe prepares himself spiritually for his task, directing his thoughts to God and ritually washing his hands. He does not work from memory, but checks each letter from a special book with perfect text. He will often say each letter loudly while he is working.

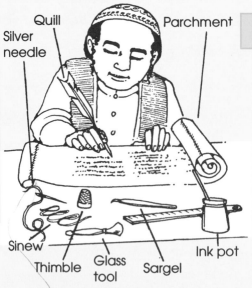

The scribe and his tools

Quill — Silver needle — Parchment — Sinew — Thimble — Glass tool — Sargel — Ink pot

Activities

- Ask the children to copy the passage in their best handwriting, leaving the name of God till last. Emphasise the idea of taking time and care to avoid mistakes and do something well.
- The children could consider what qualities are necessary in a scribe, like patience, tidiness and carefulness.

Developments

- Invite a Jewish person to talk to the children about the Torah and what it means to them.
- Ask them if they do any activities that require great care and attention, for example making a model or painting a picture.

The work of a scribe

- Choose a passage from the Torah and write it as beautifully and carefully as you can.

Remember!
Don't make any mistakes!

Remember!
Save the word God for last!

- Here is a scribe's workbag.
- Draw the tools it might contain.

Thorn

Glass

Needle

Thimble

Quill

Ink

Parchment

Sinew

Birth – Ideas Page

Aims

- To understand the birth and naming ceremonies of Jewish tradition.
- To reflect on the significance of a new baby to a family and community.

Some Hebrew names

Background

Jewish people consider a new baby to be a gift and a blessing from God, and part of a community spanning thousands of years. Anyone whose mother is Jewish is automatically part of that community. Jews believe that children should be aware of their faith and there are ceremonies that mark significant stages in their lives. At birth, the **synagogue** often holds a service of thanksgiving and dedication. When boys are born, **Brit Milah** or circumcision occurs at eight days old. It is a sign of the covenant made between God and Abraham and is the mark of a member of the Jewish faith. He is given his name at this ceremony. When a girl is born, on the first **Shabbat** after her birth, the father announces her name in the synagogue and a special prayer is said.

Jewish children may be given several names, including Hebrew and Yiddish names. This signifies that they belong to the Jewish community. The names are often taken from the **Torah** and from family tradition. Usually the first names will include reference to the father or mother, for example, David Ben Michael means David, son of Michael and Esther Bat Anne means Esther, daughter of Anne. Other popular names include Daniel, Joseph, Simon and Samuel for boys and Rebekah, Sarah, Ruth, and Rachel for girls.

Starting points

- Discuss with the children what happens when a baby is born. How do people prepare for a new baby? How is it welcomed into the family? How do families decide on a name?
- Ask them how other members of the family might feel when a new baby is born, such as parents, grandparents, brothers and sisters.

Things for a new baby

Activities

- Design the outside and inside of a card to welcome a new baby to a Jewish family.
- Talk about what pictures might be appropriate for the front. They could reflect Jewish tradition – the Star of David, a scroll, an eternal light or a menorah. What words might be appropriate for the inside of the card? The children could look up some Jewish names in the Bible for ideas.

Developments

- Collect cards that were made for the birth of a baby and make a display.
- Ask the children to write about a birth that they remember, or what they know about their own birth.
- Ask them to find out why they were given their names. Are they family names or favourite names? Did they have a special ceremony when they were born?

Welcome for a new baby!

The Goldman family have just had a new baby.

● Design a card to send to congratulate them.

● Suggest some names they could give their baby.

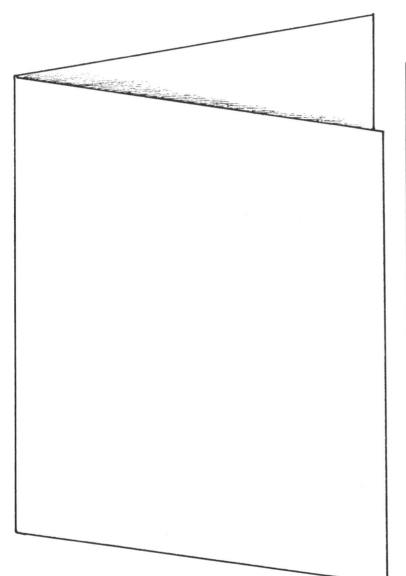

Boy	Girl

● Write down a short poem. This could go inside your card.

NOW

_____

_____

_____

_____

_____

Bar and Bat Mitzvah – Ideas Page

Aims

- To focus on the children's attention to Bar Mitzvah as a rite of passage in Judaism.
- To consider the notion of growing up and what this means in terms of new responsibilities and opportunities.

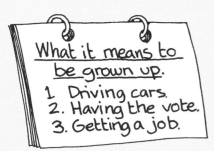

What it means to be grown up.
1. Driving cars.
2. Having the vote.
3. Getting a job.

Starting points

- Talk to the children about growing up and the different ages when new things happen, such as starting school.
- Ask them to think about being 'grown up'. What does it mean? When is a person 'grown up'?

Background

The age of adulthood in Judaism is recognised as the time when a child can understand and obey the Ten Commandments. A boy is then called **Bar Mitzvah**, meaning 'son of the law', and a girl, **Bat Mitzvah** or 'daughter of the law'. It is an important time for boys and girls and a special ceremony takes place for boys after their 13th birthday and for girls after their 12th birthday. There is lengthy preparation for the service, during which the child learns sections of the **Torah** in Hebrew. During the ceremony, the child reads from the Torah scrolls. Thereafter, the child is considered an adult within the faith and can take part in services (a boy can be counted as one of the ten men, which is the minimum number for worship), and wear the symbolic clothing of Judaism. After the Bar or Bat Mitzvah ceremony there is often a big party and the child receives presents from family and friends. The objects in the box below might be appropriate as gifts for the Bar Mitzvah.

Kippah (also known as yamulkah or capel), the head covering worn during prayers and Torah study as a sign of respect in the presence of God. Some men wear it all the time.

Tefillin (or phylacteries), small leather boxes containing scriptures. They are tied to the forehead and upper arm for morning prayers on weekdays.

Tallit prayer shawl, a four-cornered garment with fringes tied into 613 knots representing the laws of the Torah.

Siddur (which literally means 'order'), daily prayer book.

Activities

- Discuss special occasions with the children. What do they consider to be special occasions and how do they prepare? What happens and what are their feelings about the occasion?
- Discuss how a Jewish boy might prepare for his Bar Mitzvah, for example learning a Torah passage. What thoughts might he have about his new role and the ceremony itself?
- Talk about the special things on the sheet which a boy might receive on this special occasion. Ask the children to draw these items on the picture of the boy.

Developments

- Ask the children to write about a special day in their own life.
- Ask them to write a page in a Jewish boy's or girl's diary after a Bar or Bat Mitzvah. Encourage them to think about how he or she might feel about the day.

David's Bar Mitzvah

David has had his Bar Mitzvah ceremony.

- Draw on David the items he could wear or hold when he prays.

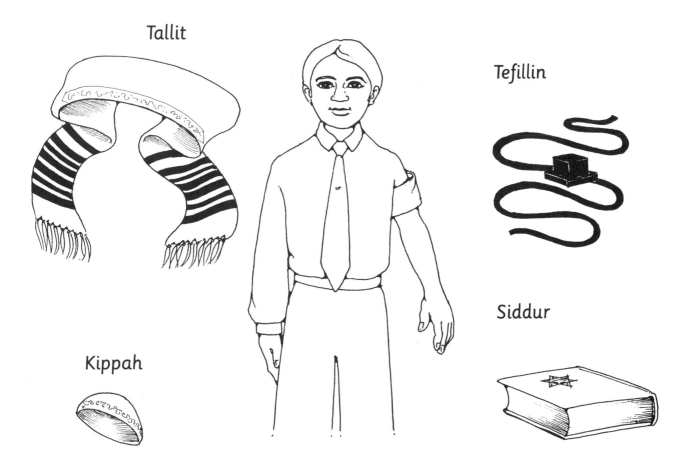

Tallit

Tefillin

Kippah

Siddur

- What would be a good present to give David on the occasion of his Bar Mitzvah?

- David is considered an adult in his religion. In what ways do we show that we are growing up:

At home? _____

_____

At school? _____

_____

With our friends? _____

_____

Weddings – Ideas Page

Aims

- To introduce the children to some of the traditions surrounding a Jewish wedding. Like traditions in other religions, marriage is surrounded by many symbolic actions.
- To consider the symbolism of the events.
- To consider the serious commitment that marriage involves.

Background

The institution of the family is important within Jewish tradition. A Jewish wedding is therefore a serious and a happy occasion, as it marks the beginning of a new life and a new family. The ceremony usually takes place in the **synagogue**, under a special canopy called a **huppah**. This is a symbol of the home the couple will share together when they are married. The service is led by the **rabbi**, who reads from the Ketubah – a document that defines the rights and obligations of marriage. During the service, the couple make promises, a ring is placed on the bride's finger and blessings are said. The service is followed by a party and the couple are wished 'mazeltov' (good luck)!

A Jewish wedding ceremony

I was bridesmaid for my big sister.

We had a big dinner and a dance afterwards

Goblet of wine – a symbol of sharing a life together

Ring – a symbol of eternity

Huppah (or chuppah) – a canopy used for the ceremony. The bride and groom stand underneath it. It is a symbol of the new home the couple will share.

Breaking the glass is a reminder of the destruction of the Temple and that there may be bad times ahead as well as good.

Starting point

- Many children will have been to a wedding and might enjoy recalling the occasion. Encourage them to remember the different things that happened during the day. It should be possible to obtain videos and photographs to support the discussion.

Activities

- Show the children pictures or a video of a Jewish wedding.
- Invite a Jewish person to talk about his or her experiences of Jewish weddings.
- Discuss the symbolism of the ceremony and compare it to those the children have been to.
- Using the activity sheet, the children could fill in the missing words and draw how they think a ceremony might look.

Developments

- Make a collage of a Jewish wedding on a large display board.
- Act out a Jewish wedding ceremony. The children could make a huppah.

A Jewish wedding

● Fill the missing words in the empty boxes.

At a Jewish wedding, the bride and groom stand under a _____ for the service. This is a sign that they will begin a new life together in a new home. The groom will also put a _____ on the bride's finger to show they will stay together forever. The couple will both drink wine from a _____ to show that they will share their life together. The groom will crush a _____ under his foot. This recalls the destruction of the Temple, and reminds the couple that there may be bad times ahead as well as good.

● Label the huppah, the goblet, the bride and the groom on the drawing below.

Aims

- To focus on the remembering of the dead, rather than the physical events. The topic of death is one that has to be handled sensitively.
- To learn something of the Jewish traditions surrounding death and the way in which people are remembered after they have died.

A short, fat candle is burned in remembrance

Background

Death is a solemn time in Jewish tradition. Jewish funerals are held as soon as possible after death. Burial is usual, especially in Orthodox tradition. The body is washed and dressed in white linen shrouds. The coffin is plain and there are usually no flowers or music. A service including prayers is performed in the **synagogue** before the burial. At the burial, relatives shovel a little earth into the grave. On returning home, they may receive an egg as a symbol of life.

The period of mourning lasts for a week, during which everyday tasks may be left undone, to signify the interruption of life. Relatives sit on low stools and friends and neighbours visit to offer help with everyday tasks. Some may make a little tear in their clothes as a sign of mourning. On each anniversary of the death, a candle may be lit and a prayer, such as the **Kaddish**, may be recited.

Within Jewish tradition, there is belief in an afterlife, but no detail is really given as to what this might look like. Death is seen as the doorway into the next life. Many Orthodox Jews look forward to the coming of the Messiah to set up a messianic kingdom on the Day of Judgement. On this day the dead will come alive again to await God's judgement. God's kingdom will be open to Jews and non-Jews (gentiles). Other Jews look forward to the coming of the messianic age of justice and peace across the world.

Book showing dedication (with Jewish calendar dates)

In loving memory of David Greene

Died 7th Tishri 5730

Starting points

- Read a children's story about death, such as *Badger's Parting Gifts* by Sue Varley (Picture Lion).
- Discuss what the children know about death ceremonies, such as funerals or cremations.

Activities

- Read the Kaddish prayer and talk about what it means. Who is the Holy One? What is meant by 'all Israel'? Why is there no mention of the dead person? Why does the prayer speak only of God?
- Discuss the possible answers to the questions on the activity sheet. It is important that the teacher knows the children well and avoids any unnecessary upset, as some of them may be sensitive.

Developments

- The children could write about funeral traditions they have seen or know about.
- Ask the children to write a prayer or a dedication that would be suitable for remembering someone who has died.
- Investigate memorials in the local area, such as war memorials, statues and plaques.

A time to remember

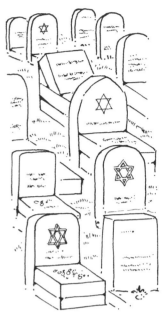

Kaddish

Blessed, praised and glorified
be the name of the Holy One,
blessed be He.
He who makes peace in His high places,
may He make peace for us
and for all Israel and say Amen.

- What do you think Jewish people think of when Kaddish is said?

  _____

  _____

- Why is it important to remember those who have died?

  _____

  _____

- Think of someone who died. What do you remember about them?

  _____

  _____

  _____

- Write your own remembrance prayer below.

  _____

  _____

  _____

  _____

Passover – Ideas Page

Aims

- To explore the symbolism behind the Passover festival.
- To understand the significance of the festival for Jewish people.
- To recognise that food is used as a religious symbol in other traditions.

Background

Passover or **Pesach** is an eight-day spring festival which begins with the house being cleaned to remove all traces of leaven (anything containing yeast or grain). This recalls the unleavened bread that the Israelites ate in their last meal before leaving Egypt. During the Passover week only unleavened bread is eaten. On the first Friday evening the family share a meal, which includes foods that symbolise the story of the Jews' escape from slavery in Egypt. A book called the **Hagadah** is used to tell the story as the symbolic foods are shared. The youngest child in the family initiates the story by asking a series of questions. The first is, 'why is this night different from all other nights?' Important themes of the festival include suffering and freedom.

The Israelites (see Exodus 5–12) were slaves in Egypt and Moses, instructed by God, asked the Pharaoh to set them free. When he refused, God unleashed a series of ten plagues on Egypt, each one worse than the last. The final plague brought about the death of the first-born in every family. The Israelites spared their children by marking their doorpost with the blood of a lamb, so that the angel of death 'passed over' them.

Starting points

- Discuss what the children understand by the terms 'slavery' and 'freedom'.
- Find an appropriate version of the story of the escape from Egypt (such as Exodus 5–12), and either read it or tell it to the children.
- Talk with the children about the special times when families gather to share a meal.

Special family meals
Passover meal
Family dinner

The seder plate

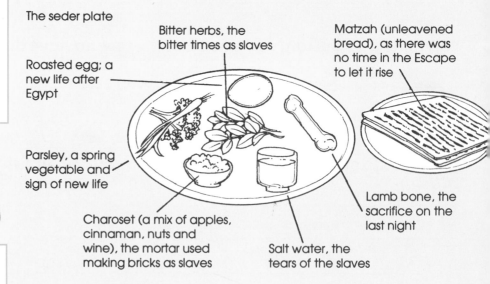

Bitter herbs, the bitter times as slaves

Matzah (unleavened bread), as there was no time in the Escape to let it rise

Roasted egg; a new life after Egypt

Parsley, a spring vegetable and sign of new life

Charoset (a mix of apples, cinnamon, nuts and wine), the mortar used making bricks as slaves

Salt water, the tears of the slaves

Lamb bone, the sacrifice on the last night

Activity

- Tell the children about Jewish families gathering to remember the story of the escape from Egypt. Talk them through the symbolism of the foods of the **seder**. The children can then identify the foods on the seder plate and match the food to its symbolic meaning.

Developments

- Make charoset using an apple, grated or chopped nuts, cinnamon and a little wine all mixed together.
- Collect the foods of the seder and use them to discuss the story with the children.
- Talk about people today who are not free, such as refugees and political prisoners.
- Ask the children to think of words that would describe a Jewish child's feelings during **Pesach**.

The seder meal

- Join the labels to the correct food on the plate.

- Then draw arrows to link each food to its symbolic meaning.

Roasted egg	Charoset	Salt water	Matzvah

Lamb bone	Parsley	Bitter herbs

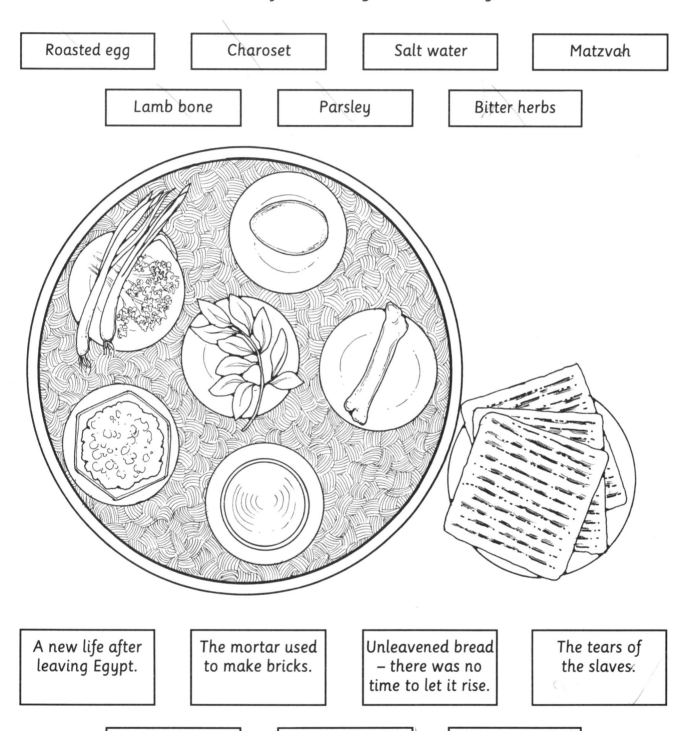

A new life after leaving Egypt.	The mortar used to make bricks.	Unleavened bread – there was no time to let it rise.	The tears of the slaves.

The lamb sacrificed on the last night in Egypt.	The bitter times of slavery.	A spring vegetable, a sign of spring and new life.

Purim – Ideas Page

Aims

- To consider the characters of the story and the reasons the characters behaved as they did.
- To understand the feast of **Purim** and its importance to Jews.
- To reflect on the importance of loyalty.

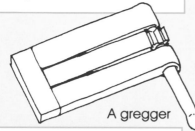

A gregger

Background

The festival of **Purim** takes place during March and celebrates Esther's triumph over anti-semitism (prejudice against Jews). Esther was the Jewish queen of King Ahasuerus (Xerxes) of Persia. Esther's cousin Mordecai worked loyally for the King and foiled a plot to kill him. However, the King's evil new advisor Hamman ordered the extermination of all Jews; Mordecai was sentenced to hang. Esther had to act to save her cousin and the Jews of Persia, and so she prepared a banquet for the King and Hamman, where she pleaded for her people. The King was greatly upset to hear of Hamman's intentions and left the room; Hamman fell at Esther's feet to beg for mercy. The King returned and, thinKing Hamman was attacKing Esther, had Hamman executed on the gallows built for Mordecai.

During the festival the story is read from a scroll called the **megillah** in the synagogue. Children try to drown out the name of the King's evil servant Hamman by banging, shouting and **shaking** rattles called greggers. Fancy-dress parties are held and gifts are given to the poor. Themes of loyalty, charity and deliverance are central to the festival.

A megillah

Starting points

- Read through the story (Esther 2–10) and decide if it is suitable to read to the children. Another version can be found in *Multi-faith Topics in the Primary School* (by Janice Webb, Cassell).
- Discuss with the children the concept of loyalty. Ask them if they have stood by one of their friends at a difficult time.

Ahasuerus did the right thing in the end.

Esther gave all to save her people.

Mordecai is brave and loyal to his people and king.

Hamman is scheming, prejudiced and cowardly.

Activities

- Read or tell the story of Esther to the children and encourage them to boo and hiss when Hamman's name is mentioned – just as Jewish children would.
- Talk about the roles of the different characters in the story, such as Esther, Hamman, Mordecai and King Ahasuerus. Make a montage.
- Ask them to match the pictures with the writing on the activity sheet. Alternatively, ask them to write in their own text; or using text only, to draw pictures.

Developments

- The children could make rattles to drown out Hamman's name. Greggers resemble football rattles, but the children could make simple ones from two yogurt pots stuck together with small pebbles inside. They could decorate their rattles.
- They could make 'hamantschen', which are three-cornered cakes made from biscuit dough, raisins and nuts. They are eaten during Purim and represent the evil Hamman's ears.
- Ask them to make hand puppets and then perform the story of Esther. Alternatively, they could make masks and act out the story as a play.

The story of Esther

The pictures and labels tell the story of Esther.
- Cut out the pictures and labels.
- Put the pictures in the right order, with the correct labels.

Mordecai warns Esther of a plan to kill the King. The King is saved.	Esther prepares a beautiful banquet, where the King offers her half his kingdom.
Esther accuses Hamman, who begs for mercy. The King thinks he is attacking Esther.	Hamman is hanged on his own gallows. Esther pleads with the King for the Jews, and the Jews are saved.
King Ahasuerus takes Esther, a Jewish girl, to be his wife.	Evil Hamman arranges to have all the Jews killed. Mordecai does not bow down to him and is sentenced to death.

Hanukkah – Ideas Page

Aim

- To understand the customs and meaning of the festival of Hanukkah for Jewish people, particularly the struggle for religious freedom.

There would be no plants or animals either.

Without light there would be no colours.

Background

Hanukkah is also called the 'Festival of Lights' or 'Dedication'. It takes place during November and December and lasts for eight days. It recalls a time in Jewish history when a Syrian king called Antiochus took control of the Temple of Jerusalem and desecrated it by sacrificing pig flesh on the altar. He ordered the Jews to forsake their own God and worship him.

A small band of Jews, the Maccabees, hid in the hills and continued to study the **Torah**. They took up arms against Antiochus' superior forces, retook the Temple and rededicated it to God. Inside the Temple, they found there was only enough oil to burn the eternal lamp for one day. By some miracle, it kept burning until new oil was found eight days later. This is remembered by the lighting of candles on each day of Hanukkah. Themes of light, loyalty, faithfulness and heroism are central to the festival.

Starting points

- Hanukkah is a festival of light. Ask the children to consider the importance of light in their lives.
- Discuss what it means to insult someone. Ask them what things might insult them or the people they love.
- Discuss 'freedom', particularly the freedom of thought and belief. Explain that the basis of Hanukkah is the struggle of the Jews against religious persecution.

Hanukkah

Activities

- Read or tell the story behind Hanukkah to the children. Discuss the themes that underlie the festival.
- Ask them to complete the circles on the activity sheet with symbolic pictures to remind them of the story. These could include a dreidel, a candlestick or a temple.

Developments

- Recreate the story on a wall frieze.
- Ask the children to make a Hanukkah candelabra. It has eight branches, one for each day of the festival, plus a 'servant' branch which is used to light the rest. This could be made as a stained glass window using black card and tissue paper, echoing the theme of light.
- The Jews had to study the Torah secretly and played with a 'driedel' (a spinning top) to disguise this. A dreidel today is decorated with Hebrew letters that remind people of the story.
- The children could make their own dreidel and play the game themselves in small groups.
- Make some potato latkes. These small cakes are made from onion and potato which is seasoned, made into spoon-sized cakes and deep fried. They are eaten during the festival.

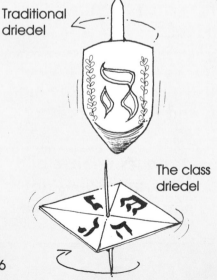

Traditional driedel

The class driedel

Hanukkah candles

- This is a picture of a Hanukkah candelabra.
- In each circle, draw a symbol which reminds you of the story of Hanukkah.

Glossary

The Ark	A curtained cupboard in the **synagogue** where the **Torah** is kept.
Bar Mitzvah	'A son of commandment'. A boy's coming-of-age ceremony.
Bat Mitzvah	'A daughter of commandment'. A girl's coming-of-age ceremony.
Bimah	Raised platform for reading the **Torah** in the synagogue.
Brit Milah	The circumcision of a young Jewish child.
Challah	Bread used during festivals and on **Shabbat**.
Haggadah	Book read during **seder**.
Hanukkah	Eight-day festival celebrating the rededication of the Temple.
Huppah	Canopy used during the wedding ceremony.
Kaddish	Prayer recited publicly by mourners.
Kippah	Head covering worn during prayer.
Kosher	'Fit' or 'proper', foods permitted by Jewish law.
Magen David	Shield or Star of David, symbol of Judaism.
Matzah	Unleavened bread used at **Pesach**.
Megillah	Scroll telling the story of Esther read during **Purim**.
Menorah	Seven-branched candelabra which is not lit because of destruction of the Temple.
Mezuzah	Scroll of the **Shema** contained in decorative box fixed on doorways.
Pesach	Festival celebrating the escape from Egypt led by Moses (also known as Passover).
Purim	Festival commemorating the saving of the Jews by Esther.
Rabbi	'My teacher'. Ordained teacher who is often a community leader.
Rosh Hashanah	Jewish New Year, when creation is recalled.
Sargel	Instrument used by the scribe to mark lines on a parchment.
Seder	Ceremonial meal eaten during **Pesach**.
Sefer Torah	**Torah** scroll, the five books of Moses.
Shabbat	Sabbath, a day of rest running from sunset Friday to nightfall Saturday.
Shaddai	'Almighty', word that adorns **mezuzah.**
Shema	Jewish prayer stating belief in one God.
Siddur	Jewish daily prayer book.
Sofer	Scribe who produces **Torah** scrolls.
Synagogue	Place of worship, study and assembly.
Tallit	Prayer shawl.
Tefillin	Small black boxes containing scriptures, tied to forehead and upper arm.
Tenakh	24 books of the Jewish Bible.
Torah	First five books of Old Testament, Jewish law or teaching.
Yad	Pointer used for reading the **Sefer Torah**.

IDEAS BANK – *Judaism*